Colors & Crystals

by Kristi Madeline Hyde

Copyright © 2020 by Kristi Madeline Hyde

All rights reserved. No part of this publication may be reproduced, stored in a retrieval system, or transmitted in any for or by any means, electronic, mechanical, photocopying, recording, or otherwise, without written permission of the publisher or author, except for the use of brief quotations in a book review.

To request permissions, contact the publisher at
freedomhousepublishingco@gmail.com.

Hardcover: 978-1-952566-12-7
Paperback: 978-1-952566-11-0
Ebook: 978-1-952566-13-4

Cover art by Kristi Madeline Hyde
Photographs by Kristi Madeline Hyde

Printed in the USA.

To all the little souls
that love finding rocks
and collecting crystals!

PINK
Love

Rose Quartz

RED
action

Red Jasper

ORANGE
balance

Orange Calcite

YELLOW
happiness

Citrine

GREEN
confidence

Aventurine

BLUE
calm

Celestite

PURPLE
harmony

Amethyst

WHITE
connect

Scolecite

BLACK
protect

Tourmaline

Rose Quartz — brings the energy of LOVE, reminding us to love ourselves by speaking kindly to ourselves and giving ourselves compassion and grace so that we can fully show up in love for others.

Red Jasper - provides a positive attitude and brightens our energy so we can take ACTION in our lives.

Orange Calcite — brings BALANCE to our emotions by clearing out fear.

Citrine — radiates HAPPINESS and abundance for all things.

Aventurine — helps remind us of our CONFIDENCE to go after our dreams.

Celestite —brings about CALM emotions to help us on our spiritual journey.

Amethyst — creates HARMONY in our lives by connecting emotional, mental & physical aspects of ourselves.

Scolecite - encourages us to CONNECT to our spirit and dreams especially in times of change.

Tourmaline — helps to PROTECT us from negative energies and thoughts.

Acknowledgements

Special thanks to my favorite crystal loving ladies from whom I have learned so much:
Judy Hall and all books in The Crystal Bible collection IG @crystaljudyhall

Heather Askinosie with Energy Muse and her book Crystal365: Crystals for Everyday Life and Your Guide to health, Wealth and Balance IG @energymuse

Magdalena with My Metaphysical Maven IG @MyMetaphyscalmaven

Thank you to Bryson's Rock Shop in Ogden, Utah for having all the beautiful crystals!
IG @BrysonsRockShop

Kristi Madeline Hyde lives in Utah with her crystal loving family. You can connect with her on Instagram @Kristimadelinehyde or search for crystals on her website www.kristimadelinehyde.com

Made in the USA
Middletown, DE
17 December 2023